BE|

The

Kindness

of a

Stranger

AN INVITATION TO HOPE

ADVANCE
BOOKS

© Ben Jack 2023

Published by Advance Books
An imprint of The Message Trust
Lancaster House, Harper Road, Sharston, Manchester M22 4RG
www.message.org.uk

The Message Trust is a company limited by guarantee, registered in
England and Wales, no. 3961183. Registered charity no. 1081467.

Unless otherwise indicated, all Scripture references are taken from NIV: New
International Version® Anglicised, NIV® Copyright © 1979, 1984, 2011
by Biblica, Inc.® Used by permission, all rights reserved worldwide.

Cover design and typesetting by Simon Baker at Thirteen Creative

Printed in the UK
ISBN: 978-1-91634-897-4

CONTENTS

'There are no strangers; only friends you haven't met yet.'

W. B. YEATS

One

STRANGERS

One of my earliest memories is of being at an outdoor market with my dad. To burn away some youthful energy and explore the sights and sounds around me, I went running away from him for a moment. I only made it a few steps before encountering the cold air of a fresh fish stall. The sudden blast of cold made me want to run back to my dad and embrace his leg for warmth, so I duly trotted back and initiated my leg cuddle. As I did, I looked up, and, to my horror, looking back at me was not the reassuring face of my dad but the confused and confusing face of a stranger. I was hugging the wrong man's leg.

Like any sensible child would, I began to scream. It was only a couple of seconds before my dad, who was literally the next man over (missed it by *that* much), took my hand and bent down to reassure me; but it felt like an eternity.

My screaming was brought on by a mixture of embarrassment, confusion, shock, and fear—of being lost and of being in trouble for doing something that felt like a big mistake to a little (often cheeky) boy. Whatever the combination of reasons, I took quite a bit of consoling, all while throwing side-eye in the direction of the strange man who would now surely haunt my dreams for decades (false alarm, I slept fine).

'Stranger Danger' is a mantra that we drum into children as a reminder to be careful not to over-trust those we don't know. A child's naivety is easily exploited, so we do what we can to protect them. And one of the simplest things is to teach children not to talk to strangers.

What such a mantra is *not* intended to do is to cause kids be distrustful of *every* person they encounter throughout life, or to grow cold towards human beings in general. And yet for some, that is exactly what happens over time as stranger danger becomes embedded into their approach to the world.

In an increasingly individualistic world, stranger danger has become a subconscious norm, thanks to a variety of factors—cold-call scammers, fake social media accounts, a twenty-four hour news cycle that constantly reminds us how horrible human beings can be, the movies, and shows we stream and more. Without realising it, we have been conditioned to treat people we don't know with suspicion; and once suspicion sets in, the stranger is not just *a* danger, but is *in* danger—in danger of never being more than a stranger to you.

At the risk of offering the most obvious definition in history, a stranger is simply a person that you don't know. We might think of a stranger as the dog-walker we pass on the street. The Amazon delivery driver who knocks on our door. The cashier at the supermarket. The obnoxiously loud phone-talker on the train. People we encounter but we don't *know* them. And yet, a stranger could just as easily be someone that we *thought* we knew but come to realise (through a behaviour, action, or opinion) that we may not know as well as we thought. Which raises the question, how well do we ever really know anyone?

It's easy to become distrustful of all but the most familiar people in our lives. Interestingly, the word 'familiar' has its roots in the word 'family'. We'll get back to that later. This distrust often plays out in subtle ways like ignoring the person sat next to us on the bus. Yet this fear can also be outworked in more disturbing ways as we potentially become disdainful of entire groups of 'strangers' from outside of our tribe. This then breeds xenophobia, racism, sexism, classism, ageism, and the 'othering' of people. The resulting alienation—or estrangement—leads in turn to the destructive devaluation and dehumanisation of fellow human beings.

As problematic as such estrangements are, they are just a symptom of the human dysfunction that comes from the ultimate estrangement we have all experienced in life. This estrangement leaves people struggling with feelings of isolation, insecurity, fear and self-loathing—merely existing in deeply unfulfilled lives, rather than truly living. It is an estrangement that goes right back to the creation of the world and the meaning of life itself.

A STRANGE EXISTENCE

I recently read an interview with fashion designer Tom Ford, who reflected:

> *Forty was the most traumatic change for me and it threw me into a depression that lasted eight or nine years. ... I'd achieved all these things that I thought*

I always wanted and then you think, 'Okay, is this it?'[1]

I've heard a similar thing expressed by people in the elite of the business world, the entertainment and fashion industries, politicians and presidents—all of whom have *fame, fortune, family, friendship, flattery* and abundant *freedoms*.

I call these things the 'little f's'. We do an equation with the 'little f's' in life. We figure that if we can add enough of them together they will hopefully equal the the big one—Fulfilment. If we are not fulfilled then we just need to keep adding and adding. Surely one day the equation will balance out to true fulfilment. These 'little f's' are not bad things in and of themselves—friendship and family are at the heart of the creation we live in. But when they become the sum total of our lives, we soon realise they don't add up to what we hoped for.

Author C. S. Lewis famously summed it up like this:

Most people, if they had really learned to look into their own hearts, would know that they do want, and want acutely, something that cannot be had in this world. There are all sorts of things in this world that offer to give it to you, but they never

> *quite keep their promise. ... If I find in myself a*
> *desire which no experience in this world can satisfy,*
> *the most probable explanation is that I was made*
> *for another world.*[2]

The Bible tells us that God has always existed, and through him all things were created. Not only has has he always existed, but God has always known perfect relationship. Christianity hinges on the unique reality that God is one and yet he is three. He is God the Father, God the Son (Jesus Christ), and God the Holy Spirit. Three Gods? No, one God expressed in the three persons of the Holy Trinity. The Father is not the Son, the Son is not the Spirit, and the Spirit is not the Father. Yet, they are inseparably one. I know, it's a mind-bender. Don't worry if you are struggling to get your head around the idea. All that matters here and now is that as a Trinity this three-in-one God has always existed in community. This reality is crucial for understanding our own existence.[3]

The Bible tells us that God is love. God has *always* been love because he has always shared perfect love within the community of Father, Son and Holy Spirit. It is out of *this* perfect relationship that God created the universe, and us human beings along with it. We are not created out of boredom, lack, or need. We are created through perfect fulfilment, relationship and love. We are created for those very same things. Creation is the overflow of God's perfect love, and what God created was very good.[4]

Better still, what God created had meaning and *purpose*.

STRANGER TO MYSELF

Are we just walking, talking space dust? Sacks of DNA reproducing more sacks of DNA? Are the sum total of our thoughts, feelings, hopes, dreams and relationships ultimately just a meaningless diversion on our passage through space and time? Or is there some purpose and meaning to this existence that transcends our here today, gone tomorrow brain function? Something that outlives our achievements and the memories we leave with others?

The Bible begins with a simple truth. You are not an accident. God has decided the universe is better off with you in it. Otherwise, you wouldn't be here. He doesn't make mistakes. He created you intentionally, out of his love and for his love.[5]

But if that's the case, I sense you thinking, *why are there so many bad people around? Did God really think the universe was better off with Hitler, Stalin, Bin Laden and [insert name of person who hurt you] in this the world?*

In the James Bond novel, *The Man With The Golden Gun*, our usually resilient hero is suffering from amnesia after the events of his last mission. Living quietly as a fisherman in Japan, events take a turn when the villains of the story use Bond's amnesia to their own advantage by brainwashing him to go back to London to kill his boss M, the head of MI6.

The manipulation of Bond to become the bad guy is a shocking twist for fans of the world's greatest spy. As a character, Bond is so clearly defined (despite some very rough edges) as the hero of the stories he inhabits. But here, with the loss of his memory comes the loss of his identity. With the loss of his identity comes the possibility of turning all of his potential for good to the use of evil.

It is not the just the world around us that can be unknown, but the world within us. Sometimes the biggest stranger in life is ourself. When we become strangers to ourselves, all the potential we have to live the life we were created for becomes confused. Where we hoped to be the hero, we end up being the villain, as our identity crisis leaves us a stranger to ourselves and the fullness of life that is available to us in relationship with our Creator.

When you walk away from God, who is the perfect source of love, light, and life, what are you walking into? Not those things. They exist exclusively within God. No, you are walking into hatred, darkness and death. The Bible tells us that this is the reality for every human being.

You might be thinking, *hold on a minute! I'm not perfect, but I'm no genocidal maniac either*. Well, first of all, I'm pleased to hear that! Still, we need to own the solemn truth about our actions in the world. We may not have killed anyone physically—but we may have killed them emotionally, with a word. We may not have caused a world war—but we may have caused a war within a household, within a relationship, within ourselves.

We have all become estranged from God. We have all turned our back on him and gone our own way. This is what the Bible calls sin. It is not simply about doing *bad things*. It is about rejecting the one who is *truly good*. By becoming strangers to God we have ensured that none of us will go through this world without leaving damage behind, or being affected by the damage of others.[6]

All the potential we have for good is rooted in the one who is truly good. Even those who don't know God can still do good things because we are all created in the image of his goodness. But the only way we could ever live in the fullness of that goodness would be to live in the fullness of the relationship we were created to have with God. As God comes into focus, so too do we.[7]

To put it another way, if you want to know *who* you are, you need to know *whose* you are.

ESTRANGED FROM GOD

In the documentary film, *Three Identical Strangers*, we discover that triplet brothers were separated at birth as part of a nature/nurture experiment to see how essentially the 'same' child would develop in different nurturing environments. That such an experiment was considered morally acceptable is shocking in itself, but the outcome of the boys' lives only makes it more so. Through a remarkable series of events—two end up at the same university and, noticing the incredible similarity in their looks, discover the truth, while the third reads a newspaper article about the 'twins' and realises likewise—the boys end up reconnecting and become minor celebrities for a short season. It transpires, though, that all three of them have struggled with their mental health throughout their lives. The cost of being separated, of being estranged from each other, left a painful and costly mark. Tragically, one of the three, Edward Galland, took his own life, aged just 33.

The violence of their separation caused the brothers problems for the rest of their lives. They weren't made to be separated in such a way. And we were not made to be separated from the God who created us and designed us for loving relationship with himself. The violence of our separation from God has wrought havoc on our world and our lives. This is not how it was supposed to be.

But strangers need not be strangers forever.

Author and Ted Talk speaker Kio Stark writes in her book, *When Strangers Meet*:

> *When you talk with strangers, you make beautiful and surprising interruptions in the expected narrative of your daily life. You shift perspective. … You find questions whose answers you thought you knew. You reject the ideas that make us so suspicious of each other.*[8]

That's good advice for how risking conversations with strangers around us could enrich our lives, but it's an even better picture of what happens when we open ourselves up to a connection with the ultimate stranger in God. We discover beautiful and surprising interruptions in the expected narrative of our daily life. When we encounter God, suddenly the ordinary can become extraordinary. Suddenly, our perspective can be reframed through his. We find that things we thought we knew are reimagined, reworked and repurposed in light of his truth. We begin to realise that we need not be suspicious of God. He is not a stranger. He is in fact the only one who has made himself truly known to the world and, by knowing Him, we may also know ourselves.

Returning to the 'little f's', then. If we want the big F of Fulfilment, we need to embrace the even bigger F of Faith. In the Bible we read these words:

> *Without faith it is impossible to please God, because anyone who comes to him must believe that he exists and that he rewards those who earnestly seek him.*[9]

What the Bible means by this is that without faith—meaning trust in God—we cannot have the kind of relationship with God that we are created for. The reward

the Bible is talking about here is the reward of true fulfilment *in him*. Peace in his presence. Without faith, we
continue to be estranged from the one who created us;
the one who puts the breath in our lungs; the one who
gives purpose and meaning to life; the one who offers
us perfect love; the one who knows us better than we
know ourselves.

My friend Andrew was sleep-walking through life,
living for the weekend and struggling to connect with
his daughter, who increasingly felt like a stranger to
him. After waking up with another weekend hangover,
Andrew found himself asking a familiar question: '*Is this
really all there is?*' But then Andrew met the kindness
of God in Jesus. With new-found purpose, Andrew has
discovered a fulfilment that he had hoped for but never
really thought possible. He has even grown closer to
his daughter, as she has witnessed the change in his life.
Estrangement has been replaced by life-changing and
satisfying faith.

It is the kindness of God that makes this faith possible,
and the good news is that while God may be a stranger
to us, we are not strangers to him...

'To kindness and love, the things we need the most.'

THE GRINCH

Two

KINDNESS

On the fateful night of April 14th, 1912 the RMS Titanic struck an iceberg in the Atlantic ocean and began to sink. Within hours the ship was lost, along with the lives of more than fifteen hundred people. In the years since, countless stories of bravery and kindness have emerged as the events of that night have been remembered by survivors. Can there be a greater act of kindness from one human to another such as was demonstrated by Andrew Latimer—a chief steward on the vessel—who saved another passenger's life by giving her his life jacket, knowing it would mean his own death?

It's easy to oversimplify kindness as simply being 'nice' to someone, but according to the dictionary kindness is more than this. It is '*the quality of being generous, helpful, and caring about other people.*'[10]

There is a moment early in the story of *Les Misérables* where, recently released from prison, Jean Valjean steals the silverware of a kind bishop who had taken him in and given him shelter. The police find Valjean with the silverware and, correctly assuming he has stolen it, bring him back to the bishop. But the bishop tells the police that he had given Valjean the silverware, and adds two more candlesticks to the haul, claiming that Valjean forgot to take them with him when he left. After the police leave, the bishop tells a confused Valjean that through this act of kindness '*I have bought your soul for God*' and that by selling the candlesticks Valjean can make an honest life for himself.

The bishop isn't simply being nice to Jean Valjean. He is being *generous, helpful and caring*. He offers Valjean meaningful help with his act of kindness and it changes the course of Valjean's life. For sure, there are still plenty of ups and downs to come in the story, but this is the moment a man without hope is set onto the path of freedom.

And here is the point—true kindness will always have an interest in freedom. Through a kind act, someone could be set free from sadness, poverty, hunger, loneliness, illness, or any other challenge or affliction they might face. Through kindness, we can realise that we are not alone. There is help. There is hope. There is freedom.

Kindness is valued in this world because it isn't just something 'nice'. It is something *needed*. In fact, the greatest need the world has ever had is the kindness of God himself, which offers us the greatest freedom.

KIND HEART AND CORONET

Jesus Christ is the most influential figure in human history. Even those who don't believe he is God often admire him as a wise teacher or a good example of kindness and compassion. You would be right to affirm Jesus as an example of kindness, but if you divorce the divine from Jesus then you miss out on the fullness of the kindness that he came to offer.

If we want to move from being estranged from God and into relationship, we need to know who God is. The Bible tells us that whilst God is invisible, in his Son, Jesus, we can *see* him. Jesus is the visible image of the invisible God. The first kindness Jesus offers us is in helping us to see just who God really is.[11]

We see the compassion, mercy, grace and love that are found in God revealed in the perfect human life Jesus lived. The more we look at Jesus, the more we see God. Without knowing it, people are compelled by Jesus—not simply because his character is something we see virtue in, but because his character is something we see our destiny in. We were made for relationship with the God whose character is revealed in the person of Jesus.

The second kindness of Jesus is in helping us to see who *we* really are. Jesus' life isn't simply an example of what a charitable, kind, or good person should look like in this world. His life displays the full extent of what it means to be truly human by showing us our true purpose—to love God above all else. Through Jesus' life we see who we can be as those who don't just know about God, but trust in him above all.

And the third kindness of Jesus is what binds knowing God and trusting him together in the fullness of relationship that we were created for. You see, that relationship is not possible for humanity, due to the damage of our rebellion against the perfect God. We have brought imperfection into the world that God created. There has never been a more unjust act than humanity rejecting the perfection of God, bringing chaos and death to the peace and life of his good creation.

Have you ever spoken the words, 'that's not fair'? Of course you have. You've been a teenager! When life gives us lemons, we are often not inclined to make lemonade but to lament. How could the world be so unjust? When will the person who hurt me get their comeuppance? Most of us don't watch detective shows hoping that the murderer of innocent victims will get away with it! Evil shouldn't win.

Justice demands that the guilty face the appropriate consequences. What then, is the appropriate consequence for rebellion against the King of life?

Death.

We crave justice until we are not the *victim* of injustice, but the *perpetrator* of it. Then, we get a little anxious about justice. We hope instead for grace. We ask for mercy.

We might think it nice for God just to let us off the hook, but it wouldn't be just. Instead of trivialising our sin with a cheap 'get out of jail free' card, God shows us that sin and its devastating effects will always be more costly to us than we can afford to pay. Sin leads to eternal death. We need this perspective so that we understand how bad sin is, contrasted with how good God is. His goodness is ultimately revealed in his kindness, which doesn't just demand justice but also makes the way for justice to be upheld, without humanity being doomed to inescapable death.

The forgiveness that God offers humanity represents the greatest kindness to all, since it comes at the greatest cost to him. God forgives us because someone else has taken our place of judgement. Jesus, whose perfect life meant that he did not need to face the judgment of death for his own sins, voluntarily took on himself the death that we deserve as a result of our rebellion against God.

Grace and mercy find us in Jesus Christ.

THE CROSS OF KINDNESS

Crucifixion was savage and shameful. It was designed to cause maximum pain as the victim died, as well as maximum humiliation. The cross was not only a tool of torture and death—it was a weapon of shame.

Before Jesus got to the stage of having nails driven through his wrists and feet to affix him to the wooden beams of the cross, he was scourged within an inch of his life with a specific kind of leather whip that had metal balls and bits of broken bone attached to it. This whip was designed to quickly remove flesh with each lashing. Such was the savagery of the process that his bones would likely have been exposed through the torn flesh. Many didn't survive this part of the punishment.

Jesus was stripped naked, beaten, mocked, spat upon, and had a crown made from weaving together long, sharp thorns forced onto his head. He was then made to carry his own cross through the streets of Jerusalem. Once at the place of execution, Jesus was laid on the cross, the nails were hammered into his wrists and feet, and the cross was hauled upright, leaving the whole weight of Jesus' body suspended on those nails.

While playing football a few years ago, I attempted to block a shot only to take the full force of an opposing player's swinging foot upon my own. I still remember the *excruciating* pain as the ligament in my ankle tore. The word 'excruciating' probably makes us all shudder a little as our minds go to a moment when we too have experienced a horrible moment of pain. Yet perhaps you didn't know that this word was invented to explain the unique pain experienced on the cross. Crucifixion was so painful that there wasn't a word adequate to describe it. So, the word *'excruciating'* came into usage, literally meaning *'out of the cross'*.

Jesus hung upon the cross—naked, exposed, bloodied and bruised—until his body could no longer sustain life. Whether through blood loss, suffocation, heart failure, or due to the spear that was thrust into his side—which must have pierced his heart for blood and water to flow out, as is described in the Bible—Jesus eventually died.[12]

You might be sceptical of these events. Perhaps they are the invention of Christians who want to make an emotional case for why you should take Jesus seriously. But both the process of crucifixion, and Jesus' experience of it, are the claim of history, not Christianity. Historian Tom Holland tells us:

> *There is no reason to doubt the essentials of this narrative. Even the most sceptical historians have tended to accept them.*[13]

You can take the cross of Christ seriously, not because a Christian wants you to, but because history compels it.

I remember hearing late US comedian Bill Hicks mock Christians for wearing crosses as jewellery in one of his stand-up shows. He made the point that, when Jesus comes back, surely the last thing he wants to see is any of his people wearing the torture device that killed him. In truth, it took the church a few hundred years to get comfortable depicting the cross in art and as a symbol of hope, because it was indeed so utterly shocking. But after the Roman emperor Constantine outlawed crucifixion in the fourth century AD, and there was a distance from those who had seen the shock and shame of crucifixion first-hand, slowly the cross of Christ began to be depicted in art, jewellery, and, more recently, tattoos.

Christians wear crosses today precisely because the cross was *supposed* to represent horror and humiliation. However, in the death of Christ the cross was turned into a symbol of hope and healing. Christians wear the cross as the ultimate symbol of God's loving kindness to us—it is not worn in embarrassment, but as invitation. The horrific consequences of our estrangement (our sin) have been dealt with in the horror of the cross. Now, instead of horror, there is hope. It might not make as good a punchline for a comedian, but it makes for a much better reality for each one of us.

But Jesus' death is not the end of the story.

A NEW KIND OF LIFE

On the third day after his death, Jesus came back to life. He was *resurrected*.

For an ordinary man, this would be implausible, fantastical—the kind of story twist that ruins the movie you were otherwise enjoying. But the twist in the story is not that Jesus came back to life. The twist is that God came to earth in Jesus Christ. If we already know *that* twist—that God became man—we are then not so much surprised as we are delighted to see him rise again. He truly is who he says he is. He is God. And God is life.

Christianity is not about following a dead guy. A dead guy can't help you. Even living ones come up short a lot of the time. But the living God? Well, that's a different story. The living God, Jesus Christ, offers us forgiveness—a way back to the Father. He gives us true life.[14]

The Bible puts it this way:

> *In his great mercy God has given us new birth into a living hope through the resurrection of Jesus Christ from the dead, and into an inheritance that can never perish, spoil or fade.*[15]

The Bible uses here the image of new birth, or being born again. That is, a chance to start this life over, this time with God in his rightful place as the centre of all that we are. Jesus doesn't offer forgiveness for our rebellion only to then leave us in the same mess we were in before. He offers us hope for a new life by sharing in his new life.

This new life is found in the invitation of Jesus to deny ourselves, take up our own cross and follow him. Jesus doesn't mean for us to be affixed to a wooden cross, as he was. He uses this image as a way of saying that we are to give up our life—our right to live as we please—and to pledge allegiance to him as the exclusive King of our lives. As we 'die' to the old way of estrangement, we can be born again into the new life of relationship with our God. Where we were once enemies through our rebellion, we have been made friends with the King. The resurrection hope Jesus offers is that no matter how broken, messed up, difficult, or painful our lives may be, a new, good, and eternal beginning is available in him.[16]

The penalty of our sin has been paid by Jesus' death. The power of death is defeated by his resurrection. Now, instead of carrying the burden of our sin, we have been *set free* to *live free* in his righteousness—*the perfect moral goodness, purity, worthiness and integrity of God*—by dying to our old life and being born again as a new creation.[17]

Have you ever been denied entry somewhere because you are wearing the wrong thing? I was recently turned away from an airport lounge for being dressed too casually (tracksuit bottoms seemed reasonable attire for a twelve-hour flight), leaving me frustrated and unrested on an already uncomfortable journey.

This is the picture that the Bible presents of the problem of our sin, if we are to enter into relationship with God. Our imperfection cannot be present in his perfect kingdom, for then it would be as imperfect as this compromised creation. As we approach God and hope to be accepted into his perfect kingdom, we have but one hope—that instead of being dressed in the dirty clothes of our old sin, we are instead dressed in the righteousness and purity of his Son, Jesus.

This is the dress code of God's kingdom. We cannot provide this dress ourselves. But, through faith, as we declare and live out the reality that God alone is our King, we are dressed by him in the clean clothes of his righteousness. The amazing reality is that all who respond to Jesus' invitation can be 'saved' and inherit the kingdom of God. And in this kingdom, the presence of sin, and all the suffering it brings, will be no more.[18]

Whether we are struggling with great pain, or have lost ourselves in great comfort, the kindness of God is available to all who recognise that, through Jesus, we can know God and be restored from estrangement to friendship with him. Through the cross, we can be forgiven. Through Jesus' resurrection, we can live as he lives. God offers us a new life—a new heart. In exchange for the dead, corrupted heart of our rebellion, he gives us in return his own living heart of righteousness.[19]

My friend Sam has a congenital heart condition that means she needs a heart transplant. Life had become such a struggle for Sam that she decided it was no longer worth fighting for. She removed herself from the transplant list, saying, '*I didn't see the point in living any more.*' But then Sam met the kindness of God in Jesus. Sam's life has been so impacted that not only has she gone back onto the transplant list, she now spends her days telling others that true life is found in Jesus. God has given Sam the new heart she needed most.

None of us is yet perfect. But, in relationship with Jesus, we are in step with the one who is. The one who, instead of offering condemnation, gave his life for us so that we might be transformed from our sinfulness into his righteousness. From death to life. From estrangement to the fullest version of relationship.

Family.

'Tennis is just a game, family is forever'

SERENA WILLIAMS

Three

FAMILY

Family can be complicated. Most of us can name at least one family member who is a bit of a challenge in some way. Or, as the old joke goes, if you can't think of one, it's probably you! Whilst we may wish we could pick and choose some of our family members, the truth is that, even when we are estranged from some in our family, they are still, by blood at least, family.

As one well known proverb tells us: *blood is thicker than water*. Family often trumps other relationships and priorities. If you've ever seen a gangster movie, they usually revolve around absolute loyalty to 'the family', which is certainly true of the greatest of them all, *The Godfather*.

By the time of the (not nearly as good) third Godfather movie, Al Pacino's main character, Michael Corleone, has realised that his gangster lifestyle leads only to chaos and death. He *almost* finds a way to cut ties with the family business and escape the violence that has defined his life. But, at the eleventh hour, his plan falls apart. In typical Pacino dialled-up-to-eleven acting style, he cries out in anguish,

> *'Just when I thought I was out, they pull me back in!'*

Back when I was DJing late into the weekend nights in bars and clubs, it often struck me how clearly people were looking for an escape for a few hours—an escape from reality. I get it. Reality is hard. Violent at times, even. There are exams to take, bills to pay, projects to complete, relationships to navigate (those difficult family members again!), and more. Reality can wage a costly war on our emotional health and mental well-being long before we experience any physical harm. So why shouldn't we take the opportunity to escape for a few hours? Dance, drink, flirt, indulge—and if that doesn't fill the life-tank with enough good times to get you through the rigours of a hard week of reality ahead, then take it to whatever excess is needed to hit that fulfilment high until the next weekend.

And yet, the regret and remorse that so often linger the following day suggest that escaping reality has one major drawback: that in returning from escape you find reality is an even harsher place than when you left it.

Just when we thought we were out, reality pulls us back in.

And it hurts.

BELONGING IN THE FAMILY

We can all benefit from a good hobby—a bit of Netflix, or Playstation, for a few hours, to switch off from the stress of life. Or a week on the beach to reset. In fact, God was the one who came up with the idea of us taking rest! Right there, in the ten commandments God gives to humanity to keep us on the right side of the moral highway, alongside being commanded not to kill or steal from each other, we are given an equally important commandment: to give an entire day a week over to proper rest.[20]

Rest is good, by God's design, and is another mark of his kindness and care for us. It's so easy to see the commandments as merely a list of rules to follow and miss what they tell us about God's character. The commandments show us that, like any good parent, God wants to set a framework for his children to thrive within. But it's even better than that, because God is not just any parent, doing their best to figure out how to raise their kids and making mistakes as they go. No, God is the perfect Father who provides a framework not simply to keep us behaving the right way, but by which we can *know* him.

Rest is good, then, but escaping reality can be a problem. It often just becomes another version of running away from the relationship with God we were created for. Rather than escaping reality, our hope of fulfilment is found in discovering that we actually *belong* to reality.

In the early nineties, my sister saved up all her pocket money with one very special purchase in mind: a shiny new Nintendo Game Boy—the coolest gadget in the world at the time. My sister treated that Game Boy like it was the most precious thing in the world. So, when mum and dad insisted that little brother should be allowed to borrow it for the coach ride of his school trip, the hesitation was understandable. Graciously, she allowed me to take it, as long as I looked after it (uh oh!).

A week later, I proudly returned from the school trip with a bag of shells and rocks from the beach for my mum. I then reached into the same bag to retrieve the Game Boy for my sister. It turns out that rocks and a Game Boy screen jostling around together in a bag aren't a match made in heaven. My sister still hasn't forgiven me.

The Game Boy was in good care with my sister. It cost her a lot and therefore became her prized possession. She never would have recklessly put it in a bag of rocks like silly younger brother who hadn't spent a penny of his own money on it.

Ironically, we are often reckless with our lives as we try to give them value. But the Bible offers us a better reality.

We belong to God, who has paid the highest price possible for us. He has given the life of his own Son, Jesus, so that we can live. We can trust him with our lives. He is not reckless with us, but caring, attentive, trustworthy, and faithful, in bringing us into the loving care of his perfect family—the reality we were created for. We are his prized possession and he is perfectly responsible with our lives.

Jesus says, '*Come to me all of you who are weary, hassled, harassed, overwhelmed, anxious, confused, stressed, and burdened, and I will give you rest.*'[21]

Instead of hopelessly escaping the stress of a broken reality, we can find rest by belonging eternally to the Perfect One.

ADOPTED INTO THE FAMILY

I was chatting with a friend recently about all that he and his wife needed to do to make the adoption of their now-daughter happen. The time, money, and emotional investment that went into bringing a little girl into their family was huge. I said to him jokingly at one point, '*Wow, are you sure it's worth all that effort?*'—to which he responded by getting his phone out to show me a picture of a happy, smiling, beautiful little girl, before saying, '*You tell me.*'

The Bible tells us that God has adopted us into his family at not just a huge cost to himself, but the greatest cost in all of the universe: the giving of his own Son, Jesus, upon the cross.[22]

From the earliest days of humanity, we have needed to huddle together to survive on this harsh planet; and from the earliest days of the internet, we've been seeking out like-minded people in chat rooms for the same reason. Technology might change, but human need basically stays the same. Today, for good or for ill, every sub-culture (and sub, sub, sub-culture) is represented online. People can search out *their* community like never before in an attempt to be seen and known in that special way we sense only 'our tribe' can see and know us. We once needed our tribe to ensure we could be fed physically and work together to fight off existential threats. Today, our tribal instincts are more likely to be about feeding each other psychologically and fighting off emotional threats. Either way, the tribe is a way to at first survive, and then thrive, through community.

The community of God is a family. He created humanity out of the overflow of his love, to share with us something perfect in order that we might delight in his love as we delight in him.

The good news, the amazing hope we have, is that as we respond to the kindness of God we become strangers no more. We don't just become *familiar with* God, but the *family of* God. Through Jesus, we move from insecurity about our place in this world to a firm foundation of our place in God's family. By the power of God's Holy Spirit, he works in our weakness to reveal his strength.

It all starts with realising that although we have run away, we can come home because of what Jesus has done for us to restore our relationship with the Father.

A FAMILIAR STORY

Jesus told a lot of stories to help us understand who God is and the hope we have of relationship with him. Probably the most well known of these is the story of the lost son.[23]

It goes like this...

A son goes to his father and says, '*Dad, it would be better for me if you were dead. If you were dead, I would have your money and then I would be truly free to live the life I want to live. So please either die, or give me my inheritance now so that I can be free to live.*'

The father is heartbroken. But knowing that true love cannot be coerced, he gives the son his inheritance.

The son heads off to the bright lights and endless opportunity of the city. He spends and spends in a quest to fulfil himself. If it can be bought, he buys it. If it offers fulfilment, he tries it.

But no matter how much the son buys, or how many experiences he samples, there is always a nagging feeling that something is missing. Whenever these feelings begin to overwhelm, the son reaches into his wallet and spends away the dissatisfaction and insecurity.

Until one day, when the familiar feelings of un-fulfilment rise, but his wallet is empty. The son, realising he has wasted his inheritance on things that don't fulfil, begins to panic. How will he distract himself from the pain of reality when he has no money to buy himself an escape?

There's a famine in the land (perhaps Jesus would have used a pandemic to make his point today), so not only does the son have to wrestle with emotional discontent, but an empty stomach as well. He becomes physically *and* emotionally malnourished. He finds the only work he can, on a farm cleaning out a pigsty, which leaves him covered in filth and no better off than he was before.

One day, while looking longingly at the pigs' food, the son came to his senses.

'*Wait, my father is a rich and good man who hires servants and treats them far better than I am living right now.*'

Knowing that there was no way to return home as the son he was, perhaps the kindness of his father might allow him to come back as a hired servant, even though he was undeserving of the privilege.

And so, the son set out on the road home—alone, insecure, and terrified of the rejection he might receive from his father. Not far from home, and playing these things over in his mind, the son saw a figure running down the road towards him. He instantly recognised the man. It was his father.

Fearing he would not have time to get his words out before his father got close enough to chase him away, the son seized his moment and in desperation began to shout,

'*I'm sorry! I know I can't come back as your son...*'

But before he could finish what he was saying, the father had wrapped him in the most loving embrace he had ever experienced. Pulling away to look at his father's tear-strewn face, the son was confused about the welcome he was receiving. How could his father greet him in this way after his family-severing actions?

The father took the robe off his back and wrapped it around his son, bringing him into the warmth of his provision. The father then took off the family ring from his own hand and placed it upon his son's finger. The son knew what this meant, even though he couldn't understand the grace it revealed. The son was not coming back simply as a servant, but as a son.

'*Tonight*,' the father said, '*we will have the greatest celebration the world has ever known. For yesterday my son was lost, but now he is found. He was dead, but now he is alive.*'

FAMILY TIES, FAMILY SIGHS

Jesus told this story so that all who heard could know that despite becoming lost, there is a way back into the family of God for all of us. Through trust in Jesus, we can turn from our estrangement, be forgiven, and be adopted as the children of God we were created to be. Where we were lost and dead, we can be found and live.[24]

For a family to work there needs to be forgiveness. When a family member gets it wrong (and we all do), without forgiveness there is no way forward. The problem is, we struggle with forgiveness today. As I look through my social media accounts, I see everything from the deeply profound to the utterly banal being posted and discussed. But I also see a lot of hatred, a lot of shaming, a lot of self-righteousness that seeks to pull others down in order to lift its own virtue up. When people make a mistake, forgiveness is not always easily found. But judgement, condemnation and—to use a term of the day—cancellation, often are.

The Bible has a lot to say about forgiveness. That we need it. That we are lost without it.

Getting lost can be a horrible feeling. For the brief moment I couldn't see my dad after hugging the wrong leg in the marketplace, I was overwhelmed by *lostness* as much as embarrassment. It's one thing to experience the unpleasantness of being lost in an unfamiliar location (how did we live without google maps?). It's another thing entirely to feel lost within yourself, or in relation to your place in this world. From bookshops to social media, we are bombarded with content that promises to help us 'find yourself'. The fact that we produce more and more of this content suggests that whilst help is needed and consumed eagerly, it might not actually be working.

Lostness comes from estrangement. When we don't know our Creator, we do not know how to be the created. Whatever virtues self-help might have, in the end it will not navigate us from the reality of our lostness to truly being found. Only the kindness of God can do that. To be found, we need to be forgiven.

Forgiveness involves more than just saying sorry. It involves changing direction. There is a special word the Bible uses to describe this action—to change direction from the path we are on and turn back to God. It is the word *repentance*.

Back on the Titanic, just before the ship hit the iceberg, it was spotted by one of the lookouts, a young man called Frederick Fleet. Tragically, Fleet didn't have binoculars with him that night. By the time he spotted disaster looming and the infamous cry of 'Iceberg, right ahead!' echoed out, it was too late for the ship to change direction and avoid catastrophe.

The good news for us is that though there may be icebergs ahead in our lives that will lead us to disaster, it is not too late for us to change direction. Even if we have already collided with a few icebergs of life and feel like we are taking on enough water to sink, there is hope in the kindness of God. There is a lifeboat that we can board to rescue us. There is nothing that God can't forgive, if we are sincere about changing course from estrangement to relationship with God, through Jesus. The lifeboat is the hope of what we call the gospel, a word that means 'good news'. The good news about our hope in Jesus.

Frederick Fleet didn't have the binoculars he needed to see the problem ahead, but God has provided us with the Bible to be our binoculars, to show us where the icebergs of life are and how we can navigate through them by knowing him. And also to be our compass, so that we would not be lost, but find our way home.

My friend Theresa was struggling to forgive herself for the mistakes she had made in life, and to forgive family members for acts of betrayal against her. Living without joy, Theresa says, '*I was consumed with resentment and guilt.*' But then Theresa met the kindness of God in Jesus. As she discovered the forgiveness and grace of God, Theresa was able to forgive herself and those around her. Instead of resentment and guilt, Theresa now lives with a new joy and peace in the family of God.

According to the well known proverb, *you can choose your friends but you can't choose your family*. But God does choose his family. He chooses us. He doesn't have to adopt us and bring us into his love—he chooses to. When we turn around from our estrangement and come home, he welcomes us back through faith in Jesus. He calls us sons and daughters and gives us an eternal inheritance of perfect peace and joy that we don't deserve.[25]

In light of such grace and kindness, we might insecurely ask God, 'Do you really want me in your family?' God would no doubt respond by pointing to Jesus upon the cross—the greatest act of love the world has ever seen—before saying, '*You tell me.*'

Just when we thought we were out, God lovingly pulls us back in.

'I still believe that love is the most durable power in the world'

MARTIN LUTHER KING JR.

Four

LOVE

Once, in Tokyo, I discovered a vintage shirt in a second-hand clothing store that was selling for around £100. When I looked at the label inside the shirt, it revealed the brand name of a popular UK supermarket chain. It was about as vintage as my breakfast that morning! You could purchase the same shirt in the supermarket for less than £10. So, which of those two prices is a truthful reflection of what that shirt is worth? Your answer will probably depend on whether you are buying or selling!

How, then, do we judge the value of ourselves or another person? Is it really as subjective and trivial as that of a shirt being sold in contrasting clothing stores? Our instinct tells us otherwise. And the Bible agrees.

God's response to our questions of value is to show us just how much value he places on us. God sends his Son, Jesus, to live the perfect human life—the life each one of us was created to live before we estranged ourselves from him—and to take our place of death upon the cross. If we judge how much we are loved by the value of the gift we receive from that love, we would see that God's love is the greatest. God could not love us more than to give us his most precious possession, his own eternally beloved Son, Jesus, the greatest treasure in all eternal existence.[26]

In God's love we find everything we hoped love could be. We find the virtues of love—care, kindness, compassion, sacrifice, intimacy, grace, faithfulness—that we long for. When we discover and accept this love, it changes us. As Victor Hugo, author of *Les Misérables*, attests in his great novel:

> *The supreme happiness of life is the conviction that we are loved; loved for ourselves, or rather, loved in spite of ourselves.*

God loves you perfectly, not because you deserve it, but because he *is* love and he created you to know and respond to his perfect love.[27]

Mercy is the giving of compassion when you have the power to deal out punishment. Rather than wiping us from the face of the earth for our rebellion, God makes a way for us to hear through his word, see through his people, experience through his presence, and respond to his love through his gospel. When putting our trust in Jesus as Lord, the love of God takes on a new dynamic—from *mercy* to *commitment*. God loves you, whether you trust him or not; but the effect of that love is significantly different.[28]

Mercy allows you to come home. Commitment allows you to stay eternally.

So how do we live in the love of God? Well, when Jesus is asked what the most important command from God to his creation is, he says that we are to love God with heart, soul, strength and mind—in other words, *everything we have*—and then we should love our neighbour as we love ourselves.[29]

LOVE GOD

I visited the Reichenbach Waterfalls in Switzerland with my family when I was a kid. After a short journey in a rickety mountain train, you arrive on a viewing platform where the thunderous sound and raw power of the immense falls become fully apparent. It was in this moment that I began to cry. I don't know what happened, but something about the environment, the power of the falls, freaked me out and I lost my emotional cool. I had to go and sit in the visitors' room until I calmed down. My mum stayed with me while my dad and sister ventured further up into the amazing natural wonder.

By the time we got back down to the base of the falls, I was already regretful that I hadn't managed to go to the top with my dad and sister, feeling that I had missed out on the experience. It was through no real fault of my own—sometimes life overwhelms and fear gets the better of you. Yet this isn't how God intends for us to live. He does not want for us to be held back by fear. He wants us to be secure in his power, in his will for our lives and his authority over this world. One of the most repeated commands in the Bible is, 'Do not be afraid'. This would be a cruel command if given by someone who had no authority or ability to save us from our fear and the things that make us fearful. But coming from God, it is not simply a command, but a promise:

'Do not be afraid, *for I am with you*.'[30]

This world can feel overwhelming at times. We have a choice: be overwhelmed by the world, or be overwhelmed by the love of God. One will lead to fear, anxiety and chaos. The other will lead to freedom, hope and peace. To be sure, knowing God through Jesus doesn't mean all fearful things go from our lives. It means instead that he is with us through it all. I know people who have been set free from clinical anxiety and depression by God's grace, and others who still struggle with those things. But they know they do not struggle alone. Even though some chaos remains, it is peace that wins in the end.

While we are estranged from God, what hope do we have but to be subject to the fears of this life? Where will our hope come from when our politicians fail us, the economy is unstable, our relationships are inconsistent, and we have little control over illness—and *none* over death?

But the Bible tells us to take heart, for God has overcome the world. His perfect love casts fear out of our lives as we learn to trust him in a world that offers much to be fearful about. He is a perfect leader. Not a mere politician, but the King of kings. The riches of his kingdom are not subject to fluctuating stocks and shares. He is always faithful in relationship. He has the power to heal and has won victory over death.[31]

Fear may come, but in knowing the love of God, and as we love him in return, fear does not win.

LOVE YOURSELF

Oscar Wilde once quipped,

> *To love oneself is the beginning of a lifelong romance.*

Romance—the pursuit and expression of love in relationship—can be a beautiful thing. Yet it can also bring a lot of insecurity along for the ride. Those early dates are exciting, but also full of mystery as to how the other person really feels about you. If we could just climb inside their mind and know what they were thinking …

Did I wear the right outfit? Pick the right restaurant? Should I have told that joke? (Learn from my mistakes, don't tell the joke).

Loving ourselves should be easier though. Right? After all, we *are* inside our own minds. Should not the mystery, and therefore insecurity, of romance disappear when we attempt to love ourselves?

Unfortunately, we often spend our lives lamenting rather than loving ourselves. Wishing we were someone other than we are. Taller, thinner, better looking, more talented, funnier, smarter … and on the lament goes. But, as we compare ourselves unfavourably to others, or to standards set as the bar of fulfilment and happiness by some influence in the world, we easily forget that even the most confident people around us carry insecurity in their lives. Indeed, many who are overly confident in their looks and abilities, to the point of narcissism, turn out to be the most insecure people.

At the heart of all this is a simple reality. People want to be valued and loved. They *need* to be valued and loved.

We all look for affirmation in some way. Whether it's from the amount of likes our social media posts generate, the promotion that follows our hard work at the office, or breakfast in bed on your birthday, we are all hoping for at least a little recognition—a tangible sense that we are seen, valued and worthy of love.

The Bible tells us that we have hope of love because God first loves us. Loving yourself in a healthy way means not swinging the self-love pendulum to one extreme of a narcissistic, 'I'm the perfect centre of the universe' (often covering great insecurity), or to the other extreme of, 'I'll be whatever you want, if you'll love me' (often revealing great desperation).[32]

Loving yourself means knowing the one who loves you as you are with all of your flaws and weaknesses. Wonderfully, he also loves you too much to let you stay that way. God's love transforms us to become the people he created us to be—the truest version of ourselves, by his perfect and good design.

Oscar Wilde, like so many, thought self-love begins with us. But it starts with God.

> ~~To love oneself is the beginning of a lifelong romance.~~

> *To love God is the beginning of an eternal romance.*

Not a romance that brings with it insecurity, but confidence, because whilst there are many mysteries about God to explore, there is no mystery about how valued, loved and accepted we are by him. The Bible tells us that we are fearfully—*created with great care, attention and purpose*—and wonderfully made; that God loves us and gave his Son for us; and that when we make Jesus Lord of our lives, *nothing* can separate us from his love.[33]

From this place of security we can trade our insecurities for something better: *confident hope*.

To love yourself does not mean standing in front of the mirror and declaring, 'I am the sexiest human alive!', or posting a no-makeup selfie to show you are comfortable with your natural look. It means to stand in front of God and declare, 'I am the weakest human alive. Help me!'—to come before him without the make-up of our self-sufficiency, acknowledging that we want to find comfort in the one whose grace is sufficient for us.[34]

The more we know God, his love and kindness, the more we discover that loving ourselves was never about our looks, ability, achievement or social standing in the world's eyes. It was never about the defiant and self-deceiving proclamation that 'I am enough!'

We discover that loving ourselves is about living in the eternal reality that *God is enough*.

LOVE OTHERS

I was watching a classic video game console being restored on YouTube the other day (my wife thinks I'm weird for watching stuff like that, but she watches clips of people organising their fridges, so I'd say we're even). I love seeing something considered broken and useless being put back together. The craftsmanship is inspiring, but it is the beauty of restoration-for-purpose that I find most compelling. This is such a powerful picture of how God in his loving-kindness takes all who have made a scrapheap of their destiny, and restores us to the purpose for which we were created—to know him, to be loved, and to love.

One of the truly amazing things about being known by God, and knowing him in return, is that we can cease to treat the world around us with hostility, or indifference, as strangers. Instead, we can discover our purpose of being a people who reveal the love of God to a world in need.

Speaking of video games, the best-selling game of all time is Minecraft—a game in which you explore a generated world, and then leave your mark on it. You can mine resources to craft new items, build pretty much anything you want, and create a world of your own making, within the confines of the world the game gives you.

We get into problems in this life when we try to create a world of our own making. But God invites us to serve him by helping to create the world of *his* making—to reflect the love we receive from him back into the world. God, in his kindness, has given us his Holy Spirit to live in us and help us to be the people we were created to be.

Recent research tells us that we are experiencing something of a loneliness epidemic in the West, to go along with peak depression, anxiety and suicide rates. This world is a tough place to exist! Humanity will always be susceptible to the challenge of loneliness, wherever isolation, insecurity, and inadequacy are part of our lived experience. We were created for community. And whenever, or wherever, community doesn't deliver on what we sense it should, loneliness follows.

Science speaks to the reality that human beings are biologically hard-wired for social interaction. We need it as part of living healthy and happy lives. Knowing God helps us to understand that this hard wiring is not incidental or accidental, we are literally designed by God for relationship - with him, and from there, with the world around us. In our Biology we therefore see an echo of God's creation purpose. In God's Spirit we receive what we need to live in that purpose.

My friend Jason grew up in an abusive household. Instead of love, he was exposed to horrendous violence from a young age. As an adult, Jason would describe his short temper, a penchant for fighting, and explosive outbursts of violence, as simply being '*in my DNA*'. But then Jason met the kindness of God in Jesus. After encountering and trusting in the love of God, Jason no longer has violence in his DNA, but peace. Jason has exchanged the chaos of the past for the present and eternal hope of Jesus. He now has a new nature. New DNA.

The Bible tells us that through the Holy Spirit we can become people of love, joy, peace, patience, kindness, goodness, faithfulness, gentleness, and self-control. Think about the kind of family, local community, nation and world we would live in if those things were the defining characteristics of our lives. This is the DNA of God himself. And by his Spirit these are the things that begin to come out of our lives as we know him and live for him.[35]

By God's Spirit, we can show people the community they were created for, as we reveal the community they were created by. We can show people a glimpse of the goodness of heaven that is yet to come. And, make no mistake, heaven is coming.

One day, Jesus will return to the world he impacted eternally upon the cross two thousand years ago. With him will come the perfection of God's kingdom and we will be in the perfect presence of God forever. There will be no more sorrow, pain, or suffering. Peace, goodness, and joy will be eternal. Perfect community will be restored, as all who have trusted in Jesus and wear his righteousness—the dress-code of love we all need to enter his Kingdom—receive our inheritance as the children of God.[36]

But all who have rejected Jesus will be separated from him eternally—a destiny that God desires for no-one.

LETTING LOVE WIN

The Bible tells us about the consequences of our estrangement from God which leaves us merely existing day by day and headed for eternal death. But we were not created for mere existence and death. We were created for life, and life in all of its eternal fullness. All who have breath in their lungs exist, but only those who have faith in Jesus Christ live, today and forevermore.[37]

God's love is too perfect to force a love response from you. True love cannot be coerced—it must be freely given. He will allow us to choose estrangement if that is what we desire. God will honour that choice and meet us in the end with the words, '*As you never knew me, so I never knew you.*' Even though God knows us better than we know ourselves, in the end he will treat us as the strangers we have made ourselves to him, if that is our will. We will be eternally estranged from God by our own choice—estranged from life, love and peace.[38]

But no-one needs to be estranged eternally.

Surrender to God.

We all recognise the gesture of an opponent putting two hands into the air as a symbol of surrender. But a father recognises this gesture from their child differently. It means, *daddy pick me up*.

In the gesture of raised hands we see the hope of the gospel.

God, I'm sorry. I surrender to you.

Daddy, I need you. Please pick me up.

Like a child in a crowded marketplace, we have all run from our Father and ended up holding onto the wrong things for comfort. As the cold air of suffering, broken relationships, loneliness, unfulfilled dreams, or the nagging suspicion that *there must more to life than this*, take hold, we so quickly grab onto anything we can for warmth. Yet our true Father is closer than we realise.

His kindness calls us to repentance. We can be found and come home to God's eternally fulfilling embrace.

His kindness leads us out of rebellion. We can pledge allegiance to God's eternally perfect Kingdom.

His kindness saves us from death. We can live today and forevermore in God's eternally perfect presence.

For his kindness calls us to be strangers no more.

AFTERWORD

This book is an invitation to know God. Your response to that invitation will change your life. These questions will help you to make your response:

- Do you believe that God created and loves you?
- Do you recognise that by estranging yourself from God you have sinned?
- Do you understand what Jesus has done to restore your relationship with God?
- Do you want forgiveness through trust in Jesus as Lord, to come home to the Father?
- Do you want to live for God through his grace and by the power of his Spirit?

If you have said 'yes' to these questions, why not pray this prayer...

Father God,
You are good and I want to know you.

I'm sorry that I have estranged myself from you,
Please forgive me for my sin.

Jesus, thank you for the kindness of taking my
place on the cross.
I choose to make you Lord of my life today.

Holy Spirit, help me to live fully for God as part of
his family,
To carry the love of God into the world for your
glory.

Amen

These are the first steps of knowing God. The next step is to get connected to a local church. One easy way to do this is to find a church near you hosting an Alpha course (www.alpha.org). Or, if you have a Christian friend, ask them if you can tag along to their church. Either way, be sure to ask lots of questions—especially as you begin to read the Bible (you can download the Bible free through the YouVersion app) and pray to the God who was once a stranger, but who, by his kindness, has become your Saviour, Friend, Father and King.

ENDNOTES

1 https://www.standard.co.uk/news/uk/tom-ford-interview-can-cel-culture-rethink-design-b965417.html

2 C. S. Lewis, *Mere Christianity*, Signature Classics Ed, HarperCollins; 2012.

3 Genesis 1:1; Colossians 1:15-17; Matthew 28:19; 2 Corinthians 13:14

4 1 John 4:16; Genesis 1:31

5 Genesis 2:7; Psalm 139:13-16; 1 John 4:7-8; Revelation 4:11

6 Romans 3:23

7 Genesis 1:27

8 Kio Stark, *When Strangers Meet* (TED), Simon & Schuster UK; 2016.

9 Hebrews 11:6

10 According to the Cambridge English dictionary. The Oxford English dictionary expresses it similarly as: *the quality of being friendly, generous, and considerate.*

11 Colossians 1:15

12 Matthew 27:32-56; Mark 15:21-41; Luke 23: 26-49; John 19:16-37

13 Tom Holland, *Dominion: The Making of the Western Mind*, Little, Brown; 2019.

14 1 Corinthians 15

15 1 Peter 1:3-4

16 Matthew 16:24-27

17 Psalm 11:7; Psalm 34:8; Psalm 145:5-7; Matthew 6:33; Mark 10:18

18 2 Corinthians 5:2; Ephesians 4:22-24; Philippians 3:9

19 Romans 5:1-11

20 Exodus 20:2-17

21 Matthew 11:28

22 Galatians 4:4-5

23 Luke 15:11-32

24 John 1:12-13

25 Romans 8:14-17

26 John 3:16; Ephesians 2:7

27 1 John 4:9-10;16

28 Ephesians 2:4-5

29 Matthew 22:37-39

30 Isaiah 41:10

31 John 16:33; 1 John 4:18; Revelation 19:16; Matthew 6:19-21; Psalm 145; 1 Corinthians 15:54-57

32 1 John 4:19

33 Psalm 139; John 3:16; Romans 5:8; Romans 8:37-39

34 2 Corinthians 12:9

35 Galatian 5:22-23

36 Hebrews 9:28; Revelation 1:7; 21:4

37 John 10:10; John 14:6

38 Matthew 7:23